Greenwillow Books New York

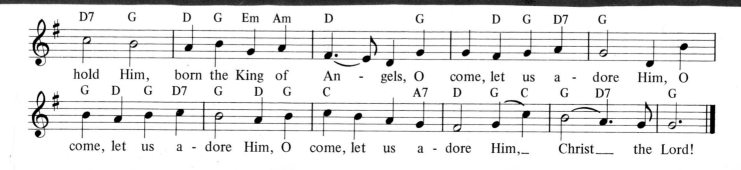

hold Him, born the King of Angels, O come, let us adore Him, O come, let us adore Him, O come, let us adore Him, Christ the Lord!

To my guardian angel

Library of Congress Cataloging-in-Publication Data
Guback, Georgia.   The carolers/by Georgia Guback.   p.   cm.
   Summary: Follows a group of carolers from house to house as they share with others the beauty of Christmas. Includes lyrics and music from the carols they are singing.   ISBN 0-688-09772-3 (trade).   ISBN 0-688-09773-1 (lib.)
[1. Christmas—Fiction.   2. Stories without words.]   I. Title.   PZ7.G9343Car   1992   [E]—dc20
90-41756   CIP   AC

bove thy deep and dream-less sleep the si-lent stars go by; Yet

in thy dark streets shin - eth the ev - er - last - ing Light; The

hopes and fears of all the years are met in thee to-night.

The — first — No - el, the_ an - gel did say, Was to cer - tain poor

sheep, On a cold win-ter's night _ that was _ so deep. No - el, _ No -

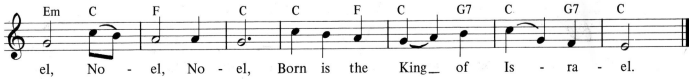

el, No - el, No - el, Born is the King_ of Is - ra - el.

AWAY IN A

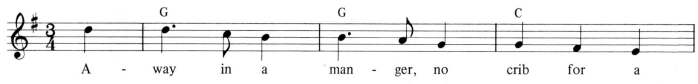

A - way in a man - ger, no crib for a

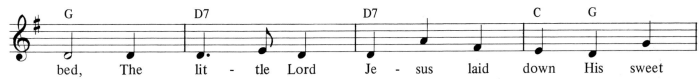

bed, The lit - tle Lord Je - sus laid down His sweet

head. The stars in the sky_____ looked down where He

lay,   The   lit - tle   Lord   Je - sus,   a - sleep   on   the   hay.

mer - cy mild,___ God and sin - ners rec - on - ciled!" Joy - ful, all ye na - tions rise,___

join the tri-umph of the skies;_ With th'an-gel-ic host pro-claim, "Christ is_ born in

Beth - le - hem!" Hark! the her - ald an - gels sing, "Glo - ry__ to the new - born King!"

WE THREE

We three kings of O - ri - ent are; Bear - ing gifts we tra-verse a -

far, Field and foun-tain, moor and moun-tain, Fol-low-ing yon-der Star.

O— Star of won-der, Star of night, Star with roy-al beau-ty bright,

West - ward lead - ing, still pro - ceed - ing, Guide us to Thy per - fect Light.

Si - lent night! ho - ly night! All is calm,

Ho - ly In - fant so ten - der and mild, Sleep in heav - en - ly

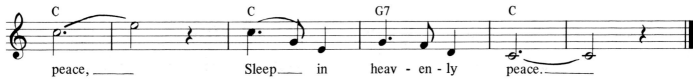

peace, _____ Sleep _____ in heav - en - ly peace.

It came up-on__ a mid - night clear, that glo - ri - ous song__ of old,___ From

an - gels bend - ing near the earth to touch their harps__ of gold; ___ "Peace

WHAT CHILD IS THIS, WHO,

What Child is this,_ Who, laid to rest,_ on Mar - y's lap_ is sleep - ing? Whom

an - gels greet_ with an - thems sweet,_ while shep - herds watch_ are keep - ing?

LAID TO REST, ON MARY'S LAP...

This, this is Christ the King, Whom shep-herds guard and an - gels sing;

Haste, haste to bring Him laud, the Babe, the Son of Mar - y.

We wish you a merry Christ - mas! We wish you a mer - ry Christ - mas! We wish you a mer - ry